W9-BHG-619

Thomas Paine and the Power of *Common Sense*

Jeremy Aldritt

NEW YORK

Published in 2016 by The Rosen Publishing Group, Inc.
29 East 21st Street, New York, NY 10010

Photo Credits: Cover DEA Picture Library/Getty Images; pp. 4, 7, 12, 17 Hulton Archive/Getty Images; p. 5 ©
North Wind Picture Archives ; p. 9 Universal Images Group/SuperStock; p. 10 Thetford, Norfolk, UK/Photo © Neil
Holmes Bridgeman Images; p. 11 Print Collector/Hulton Archive/Getty Images; p. 13 DeAgostini/Superstock; p. 15
ClassicStock.com/SuperStock; p. 19 © Interfoto/Alamy; p. 21 MPI/Archive Photos/Getty Images

Library of Congress Cataloging-in-Publication Data

Aldritt, Jeremy.
Thomas Paine and the Power of "Common Sense" / Jeremy Aldritt. -- First edition.
    pages cm. -- (Spotlight on American history)
Includes bibliographical references and index.
ISBN 978-1-4994-1768-5 (library bound) -- ISBN 978-1-4994-1765-4 (pbk.) --
ISBN 978-1-4994-1764-7 (6-pack)
1. Paine, Thomas, 1737-1809. Common sense--Juvenile literature. 2. Paine, Thomas, 1737-1809--Juvenile
literature. 3. United States--Politics and government--1775-1783--Juvenile literature. 4. Political science--
History--18th century--Juvenile literature. 5. Monarchy--Juvenile literature. I. Title.
E211.P153A438 2016
320.51092--dc23
[B]
                              2015018928

Manufactured in the United States of America

CPSIA Compliance Information: Batch #WS15PK: For Further Information contact Rosen Publishing, New York, New York at 1-800-237-9932

CONTENTS

THE POWER OF THE PEN

Thomas Paine wrote, "We have it in our power to begin the world over again." These words are from his famous **pamphlet**, *Common Sense*. He published these words on January 10, 1776.

The war between Britain and its American **colonies** had been going on since April 1775. There were many reasons why the colonists wanted their freedom from

This portrait of Thomas Paine is an engraving that was created around 1770. At the time of this portrait, Paine had not yet written Common Sense.

This hand-colored woodcut was created in 1765. It shows colonists burning a carriage in New York City to protest the Stamp Act.

Britain. The major reason was that Americans no longer thought that their wishes mattered to the British king or to the British **Parliament**. The colonists were being **taxed** to pay for the expensive French and Indian War, which lasted from 1754 to 1763.

The British had fought the French for **territory** within North America. The American colonists had fought and

died for Britain in this war. With the war over, the colonists were very angry that they were being taxed so unfairly to pay for the war. They refused to suffer taxation without representation. They refused to pay taxes on tea and on printed material. They protested the Stamp Act of 1765 and the Coercive Acts, or the Intolerable Acts as they were known in the colonies, of 1774.

King George III wanted to force the colonists to obey his laws. He sent his soldiers, the British redcoats, to enforce his policies. This eventually led to a new war. This war was the American Revolutionary War.

Many of the leaders of the colonies spoke and wrote about the justice of the **revolt**. No one wrote more persuasively about the cause of liberty than Thomas Paine in *Common Sense*. He expressed what was in the hearts of all American patriots. He defined the cause for which everyone was fighting. His 47-page pamphlet became a best seller. He sold more than 150,000 copies. That is the equivalent of 15 million copies today.

COMMON SENSE;

ADDRESSED TO THE

INHABITANTS

OF

AMERICA,

On the following interesting

SUBJECTS.

I. Of the Origin and Design of Government in general, with concise Remarks on the English Constitution.

II. Of Monarchy and Hereditary Succession.

III. Thou

IV. Of t
Reflections.

This is the title page of the 1776 edition of Common Sense printed and sold by R. Bell in Philadelphia.

TO SPEAK THE TRUTH TO POWER

Thomas Paine was one of the most courageous men of the 1700s. He wasn't afraid to write the truth as he understood it. He wasn't afraid to fight against the powerful people who ruled. He believed in the rights of the individual. He became a hero to the common people. He was an enemy of kings and those who opposed liberty and justice for all. Those people spread lies about him. They said what he wrote was illegal. They put him in prison.

Through all these problems, Paine never stopped defending the individual. Paine was very opposed to slavery. He said one of the worst things the British government did was to make the business of slavery legal.

In the spring of 1775, Paine published *African Slavery in America*. In this article, Paine condemned slavery for being unjust and inhumane. He argued that all people have a natural right to freedom.

This illustration shows a slave chained to the ground. The poem beneath this image was written by the English poet William Cowper (1731-1800).

I would not have a Slave to till my ground
To carry me, to fan me while I sleep,
And tremble when I wake, for all the wealth
That sinews bought and sold have ever earn'd.
We have no Slaves at home—why then abroad?

COWPER.

9

EARLY LIFE IN ENGLAND

Thomas Paine was born in 1737 in the small English town of Thetford. This town is 75 miles (121 kilometers) from London. Thetford was under the control of a wealthy aristocrat, the Duke of Grafton. In England in 1737, most people could not **participate** in government. Of a population of five million Englishmen, only 6,000 could vote.

This bronze statue of Thomas Paine was created by Charles Wheeler in 1964. It stands in Paine's hometown of Thetford to honor his work.

There were many debtor prisons in England in Thomas Paine's time. This illustration shows the arrival of a debtor to Fleet Prison.

Life was hard for the average worker. There were poor working conditions. Thomas Paine witnessed a lot of social injustice. Parliament passed many laws to punish crime severely. Women and children could be killed for stealing a loaf of bread.

THE EDUCATION OF THOMAS PAINE

Thomas Paine lived in a cottage near Gallow's Hill. This was the place where people were hanged for crimes. For 19 years, Thomas Paine watched people led from prison to their deaths. The injustice of British law made a strong impression on him. Years later, he asked in one of his books why only the poor seemed to be hanged.

Executed this Day before the Debtor's Door, Newgate. *To which is added*, The Copy of a moſt excellent Prayer, written and uſed by *Thomas Hunter*, during his Confinement, and is recommended to the Uſe of every Perſon.

In 18th-century England, public executions were common. This illustration shows two prisoners executed in Newgate in 1797.

This engraving, created in 1735, shows a Quaker assembly in London.

Thomas's father was a Quaker. Quakers believed in **equality**. They were against slavery, injustice, war, and killing people for committing crimes. Thomas learned a lot about justice from his father's beliefs. Thomas went to school until he was 13. He then became an **apprentice** of his father. He learned to make stays, or strong ropes, for ships' masts. After six years, he left his father to go to London.

LIFE IN LONDON AND LIFE AT SEA

When Thomas Paine came to London in 1756, it was a big city. There were 600,000 **inhabitants**. Thomas went to work for a friend of his father. This man made stays for ships, just as Thomas's father had. Thomas wanted adventure. He became a sailor on a ship called the *King of Prussia*. This was a privateer ship. These ships attacked and seized the ships of other countries. Doing this was dangerous, but the captain and crew could make a lot of money. The *King of Prussia* seized nine ships.

When the ship returned to England, Thomas left it. He had seen enough blood and death. He wanted to use the money he earned to continue his education. Back in London in 1757, Thomas attended lectures at the Royal Academy. He heard famous scientists describe many new discoveries. He also learned new political ideas.

English privateers took on the dangerous work of attacking Spanish ships. They did so because they could gain great wealth. This dramatic 20th-century illustration by Howard Pyle shows the risks.

MARRIAGE AND WRITING

Paine married Mary Lambert in 1759. They were very happy together, but unfortunately Mary died in childbirth in 1760. Paine was very sad and lonely, so he decided to change his life again. He studied to enter the profession of Mary's father. Paine wanted to be an exciseman, or a person who collects taxes. He was successful in joining this profession.

This change was a very important step in Paine's life, as it created an opportunity for him to write for a just cause. When his fellow excisemen became unhappy with their pay, they turned to Paine to write a petition to Parliament. This was Paine's first public pamphlet.

Paine was unsuccessful at getting Parliament to raise the pay of excisemen, but the pamphlet was very important. The ideas in this pamphlet would form the basis for all his future work. He argued that logic mixed with strong morals would make a just society.

Thomas Paine wrote many works and became famous throughout the world. His first published work was his petition to Parliament on behalf of excisemen.

GOING TO AMERICA

Paine met Benjamin Franklin in London in 1773. Franklin told Paine he should go to America to start a new life. Paine left England in September 1774. He arrived in Philadelphia two months later. He carried letters from Benjamin Franklin. These letters introduced Paine to important people who would help him.

There were many opportunities in America at this time. Many people were farmers. There was also a lot of trade with countries around the world. Some people were getting rich. Paine also saw the terrible practice of slavery firsthand. There were three million people in the American colonies. There were 750,000 African slaves.

Americans wanted freedom from British rule. They argued for "no taxation without representation." They protested the British Parliament's taxes: the Sugar Act of 1764, the Stamp Act of 1765, and the Tea Act of 1773. Paine understood quickly that it was strange for Americans to want freedom from Britain, while at the same time forcing African slaves to work.

This 19th-century engraving places Thomas Paine (bottom left) among the founding fathers of America. He keeps company with Benjamin Franklin, George Washington, John Adams, and Thomas Jefferson.

WRITING
COMMON SENSE

Paine became a **journalist**. He took a job writing for the *Pennsylvania Magazine*. Readers loved his style. The magazine gained many new readers. Leaders of the Continental Congress read Paine's words. He supported the rights of women. He opposed slavery.

When war began between Britain and the American colonies in 1775, Paine supported the need for independence from Britain. Many important people asked him to write a pamphlet to explain why independence was necessary.

In the fall of 1775, he wrote *Common Sense*. It became a best seller throughout the colonies and in Europe, too. He defined America as a land of liberty. He gave clear reasons to fight. He showed how the American struggle for freedom was a fight for all of humanity. He said a government existed only to provide freedom and security for people. Paine created a new language for **democracy**. He made democracy easy to understand.

THE
PENNSYLVANIA
MAGAZINE:
OR,
AMERICAN
MONTHLY MUSEUM.
MDCCLXXV.

VOLUME I.

This is the first issue of the Pennsylvania Magazine edited by Thomas Paine in 1775.

THOMAS PAINE'S INFLUENCE

Paine wrote many pamphlets after *Common Sense*. In 1776, he wrote *The American Crisis*. He wrote it to inspire Americans to keep fighting when the Revolutionary War was not going well. His words helped the Continental army to grow.

In 1777, he wrote an open letter to the British commander, Lord Howe. In this letter, Paine became the first person to call the new American country the United States of America.

Paine continued fighting for the freedom of all people after the Revolutionary War. In 1787, he went to France. France was having its own revolution against a king who did not care about his people. In 1791, Paine published *Rights of Man*. This pamphlet defended the French Revolution. It was a best seller. Thomas Paine died on June 8, 1809, in New York City. His words helped create a philosophy of democracy that exists to this day.

GLOSSARY

apprentice (uh-PREN-tis) Someone who attaches himself or herself to a master at some profession in order to learn the business.

colonies (KAH-luh-neez) Areas in new countries where large groups of people move who are still ruled by the leaders and laws of their old country.

democracy (dih-MAH-kruh-see) A government that is run by the people who live under it.

equality (ee-KWAH-luh-tee) When all people have the same rights.

inhabitants (ihn-HAA-buh-tuhnts) People who live in a certain place.

journalist (JUHR-nuhl-uhst) A person who writes news stories for a newspaper or magazine.

pamphlet (PAM-fluht) A small, thin book.

Parliament (PAHR-luh-muhnt) The group of people who are responsible for making the laws in Britain.

participate (pahr-TIH-suh-payt) To be involved with others in doing something.

revolt (rih-VOHLT) To fight in a violent way against the rule of a leader or government.

taxed (TAKS-d) To impose a tax on something or someone.

territory (TEHR-uh-tohr-ee) An area of land that belongs to or is controlled by a government.

INDEX

PRIMARY SOURCE LIST

Page 5: Original woodcut from *Our Country; A History of the United States from the Discovery of America to the Present Time with Over Seven Hundred Illustrations by Felix O. C. Darley and Other Well-Known Artists*, which was an 8-volume collection. Published by Benson John Lossing, Lossing History Company of New York in 1905.

Page 7: The title page of Thomas Paine's *Common Sense* published by R. Bell, Philadelphia in January 1776. Original edition copies are stored in the Rare Book and Special Collections Division of the Library of Congress.

Page 9: Oil painting titled *The Kneeling Slave-'Am I not a Man and a Brother'* was created by an English painter in the 18th century. It is owned by the Wilberforce House, Hull City Museums & Art Galleries, United Kingdom.

Page 13: Early engraving, *United Kingdom, England, A Quaker Assembly in London* was created in 1735. Artist unknown.

Page 15: This image, *An attack on a Galleon*, was published in *Howard Pyle's Book of Pirates*, in 1903 by Harper & Brothers Publishers, New York/London.

Page 21: The title page for the first issue of *The Pennsylvania Magazine or American Monthly Museum*, published in 1775 by Thomas Paine. Engraving by R. Aitken.

WEBSITES

Due to the changing nature of Internet links, PowerKids Press has developed an online list of websites related to the subject of this book. This site is updated regularly. Please use this link to access the list: www.powerkidslinks.com/soah/pain